From Addiction To Recovery

My Journey With Drugs

By Charles A. Brown

Table of Contents

Introduction

There was a young lady by the name of Jane. She had big plans for the future and aspirations of becoming a prosperous entrepreneur. She was on the verge of accomplishing her ambitions and had a supportive family that encouraged her to pursue her aspirations.

However, she was hindered by one thing: her drug addiction. Since she was a youngster, Jane had struggled with drug abuse, which harmed her life. She had lost friends, suffered academic failures, and even been detained for drug possession. She had made several attempts to stop but nothing seemed to work.

Jane's addiction simply became worse over time. She began abusing more potent substances and engaging in riskier actions. There didn't appear to be a way out as she continued along a dim road.

Up until one day, Jane lacked perspective. She realized that she needed to get sober to fulfill her aspirations. She was aware that she couldn't continue to let her addiction rule her life. She decided to seek therapy and start the process of recovery with the support of her family and friends.

It wasn't simple. Jane had to put forth a lot of effort to maintain her sobriety and she had to acquire appropriate coping mechanisms for her addiction. But she was committed to changing, and eventually, she succeeded.

Jane is now living a happy and healthy life. She is a wonderful role model for individuals struggling with addiction since she has accomplished many of her objectives and ambitions. Although she is aware that her road to recovery is not yet complete, she is thankful for every day that she has been sober.

The tale of Jane is one of bravery, tenacity, and optimism. It serves as a reminder that anybody can beat addiction and have a fulfilled life if they put their mind to it.

Chapter 1

Childhood Adversity

Jane's early years were extraordinarily vivid. She grew up in a little town tucked away in the gently undulating slopes of the Appalachian Mountains as the eldest of three children. Her days were full of learning, exploring, and fun thanks to her hard-working farming parents.

When Jane would go into the woods with her siblings, it was her favorite time of the day. The trio would amble around the verdant woodland, gathering wildflowers and keeping an eye out for wildlife. They would return home with a pocketful of valuables, including pebbles, feathers, and sticks.

The family would go fishing at a tiny pond close to their home. When Jane managed to catch a fish, her parents would always take her out to a nearby restaurant to celebrate. When Jane could bring home a fish for supper, she felt very accomplished.

Jane excelled in school and had a constant desire to learn. She loved learning new things and was very curious about the world. She was very interested in science and often questioned her instructor. She picked things up quickly and soon was assisting in educating her classmates about the many plant and animal species that lived around.

Jane and her siblings would tour the adjacent town on the weekends. They would visit the neighborhood library to borrow books or the local movie theater to see a film. In the summer, they would go camping or take lengthy excursions in the mountains.

A telescope was given to Jane as a birthday gift when she turned 10. She was ecstatic to be able to see the stars and was filled with awe at the thought of what may be in the cosmos. She used to lie on her back on the grass for hours, simply staring up at the night sky and wondering what was beyond.

Jane has many fond recollections of her youth. She treasured the time she spent with her family and friends discovering new things and learning about the world. She still remembers her youth and the experiences she experienced, even if she is now an adult and lives somewhere else.

Chapter 2

The Addiction

Jane was a young woman with a bright future ahead of her. She was intelligent and talented. She was a top student and had a large social circle. Up until the fatal day when she decided to take drugs for the first time, everything seemed to be ideal.

It all started with a challenge from her schoolmates. Initially reluctant, Jane ultimately caved into social pressure and decided to give it a go. She was terrified since she had heard horror tales about drug addiction, but her curiosity won out.

The encounter was first thrilling and enjoyable. She experienced an adrenaline rush and happiness she had never experienced before. She started regularly taking drugs since she believed them to be the finest sensation in the whole world.

Jane quickly began to get dependent on narcotics. Every time she had stress, anxiety, or depression, she would take them. She would also use them to deal with the stress of relationships, jobs, and education.

Jane started to lose control over time. She started to skip work and school, which affected her grades and her relationships with her family and friends. She was spending an increasing amount of time alone and abusing drugs.

Eventually, Jane was completely consumed by her addiction. She began to neglect her health and hygiene and started to take dangerous risks to get her to fix it. She was lying, stealing, and cheating to get the drugs she so desperately needed.

Jane's family and friends were horrified by her behavior and had no idea how to help her. They felt helpless and powerless as they watched her slip further and further away from them.

As days passed, Jane became more and more enamored with the drug. She started to use it more frequently and soon she found herself in a downward spiral. She was missing school and her grades were suffering, her family relationships were strained, and she was skipping meals. She was becoming increasingly isolated and was slipping further and further away from reality.

The first time she tried an illicit substance was when her friends offered her a hit of marijuana. She was nervous, but after the initial wave of anxiety passed, she found that she quite enjoyed the feeling of being high.

From then on, Jane's exposure to drugs gradually increased. Her friends began to offer her different substances, and she slowly began to experiment with them. She tried LSD, ecstasy, cocaine, and even heroin. Each time she took a new drug, she felt more and more intrigued.

2.1 Health Consequences

Janes was a young girl who had been struggling with drug addiction since she was a teenager. She had been experimenting with drugs since she was in high school, but the problem had escalated in recent years. She was now addicted to a variety of drugs, including opioids, cocaine, and methamphetamine.

The impact of her drug addiction had been devastating to her health. Her physical health had deteriorated rapidly, with her complexion becoming unhealthy and her weight dropping drastically. Her mental health had also taken a hit, with her suffering from depression and anxiety. She was also unable to concentrate and had difficulty sleeping.

Janes was aware of the harm that her drug addiction was causing her, but she was unable to break free from its grip. Her family had tried to help her, but she was too entrenched in her addiction to make any meaningful progress. She was too ashamed to seek professional help, so she continued to suffer in silence.

The impact of her drug addiction had been far-reaching. She was unable to hold down a job, so she had become destitute. Her relationships had suffered as she was unable to maintain any meaningful connection with her loved ones. Her social life had also taken a hit, as she was too embarrassed to be seen in public.

2.2 Effects on Personal Relationships

Janes was a young woman in her early twenties who had been struggling with addiction for the past few years. She had been using various drugs, including cocaine, marijuana, and opioids. Her addiction had started as recreational use, but soon became something she relied on to cope with life's daily stresses.

Unfortunately, Jane's drug use had taken a toll on her relationships and personal life. First and foremost, it had ruined her relationship with her family. With every drug purchase, she was lying to them and stealing money to support her habit. This caused a huge rift between them, with her family feeling betrayed and angry.

At work, Jane's addiction started to affect her performance. She was often late to work, or didn't show up at all. She was forgetful and unfocused, and her employer was becoming frustrated with her. This was causing her to become more and more isolated from her coworkers, and eventually, she was fired.

On the social side, Jane's friends started to distance themselves from her. She had become unreliable, and her drug use put a strain on their relationship. Her friends had started to worry about her and tried to help, but it was too late. Jane had pushed away everyone who cared about her.

The biggest impact of Jane's drug addiction was on her mental health. She had become depressed and anxious and was unable to cope with life's struggles. She was constantly feeling overwhelmed and was unable to make decisions or take action. Her addiction had robbed her of her ability to function normally.

In the end, Jane's drug addiction destroyed her life. She had lost her family, her job, and her friends. She was isolated and alone, and her mental health was in shambles. She was desperate for help but was unable to find it.

Chapter 3

The Path To Recovery

It was a long, painful trip for Jane. She had been suffering from drug abuse for some years and it was taking over her life. She had attempted to stop several times, but she always managed to find her way back to her addiction. She was in a sad place and felt like she had struck rock bottom.

One day, Jane decided enough was enough. She took the choice to get therapy and get her life back on track. She began by attending a local support group, where she was able to chat with other individuals who were battling with the same concerns. Jane felt solace in knowing she wasn't alone.

The next step was to locate a specialist who could assist her with her addiction. Jane was fortunate enough to discover a skilled therapist who specialized in addiction treatment. After numerous sessions of talking about her challenges and her plans for the future, Jane started to notice changes in her life.

With the guidance of her therapist, Jane established precise objectives for her rehabilitation. She created a strategy to gently but certainly eliminate her drug use and concentrate on good practices. She also started to search for hobbies that she loved, such as reading, drawing, and even going for walks in the park.

The toughest part of the trip for Jane was learning how to manage the cravings and desires that came with her addiction. She learned how to detect the triggers that lead her to use and how to develop healthy methods to deal with her feelings. With discipline, Jane was able to fight her urges and continue on the road to recovery.

As time went on, Jane continued to make progress in her rehabilitation path. She was able to sustain her sobriety and even began to feel more in charge of her own life. Jane was slowly but surely getting her life back and living a better, happier existence.

Jane is now a strong, independent lady who is proud of the accomplishments she has achieved. She is still working on her recovery, but she is no longer ruled by her addiction.

Chapter 4

Coping Strategy And Maintaining Sobriety

Jane had been dealing with her drug use for years, but she was determined to make a change and begin on the road to recovery. She realized that the only way to do so was to create a strong coping mechanism to assist her to sustain sober.

At first, Jane was overwhelmed by the quantity of help and resources available to her. She understood she needed to make the most of them, but she also needed to establish her coping method. Jane decided to start by developing a support system of individuals who might help her remain on track. She went out to her family and close friends and asked them to be her accountability partners. She also joined an internet support group, so she could interact with other individuals in similar circumstances.

Once she had created a solid support structure, Jane started to concentrate on her mental health. She began attending weekly therapy sessions to work through her mental concerns, and she made sure to practice self-care every day. Jane also started to meditate and practice mindfulness to help her remain balanced and connected to her inner self.

In addition to her mental health, Jane also focused on her physical health. She began exercising daily and eating a healthy diet. She even took up yoga to help her remain grounded and calm. Jane also adopted healthy habits like drinking lots of water and getting adequate sleep into her daily routine.

As Jane continued to make progress in her recovery path, she started to construct a solid set of skills to help her remain clean. She learned to know her triggers and how to handle them healthily. She also started to journal and write down her thoughts and feelings so she could stay in tune with her emotions.

Finally, Jane began to focus on her spirituality. She started to read up on spiritual practices and explore different religions and philosophies. She realized that by connecting to something greater than herself, it was easier for her to find calm and remain focused on her journey of recovery.

By adopting these coping skills into her life, Jane was able to remain sober and continue on her road to recovery. With the help of her support system and her determination, she was able to make lasting changes in her life and live a life of sobriety.

Chapter 5

Finding Redemption

There was a young lady called Jane who had been battling heroin addiction for years. She had attempted many forms of therapy, and each time she had failed spectacularly. She wanted to escape the cycle of addiction because she was sick of it.

Jane decided to try something new one day. She was aware of a program called Redemption that assisted individuals in overcoming drug addiction. Despite her doubts, she chose to give it a go.

She was welcomed by kind and welcoming personnel at the Redemption center who immediately put her at ease. They gave her an outline of the course of action and what to anticipate. Jane was impressed and decided to try it.

The Redemption program put a strong emphasis on giving Jane the knowledge and tools she needed to avoid using drugs and healthily deal with her addiction. She received instruction on how to recognize relapse-risk factors, control urges, and create a solid support network.

Additionally, the program gave her access to therapeutic activities that supported the development of new cognitive and behavioral patterns. She was able to learn how to create a solid support network and how to control her emotions healthily.

Jane started to experience optimism and hope as she moved along in the program. Her urges started to fade, and she gained more self-assurance. She was able to identify her advantages and disadvantages, which gave her the confidence to make adjustments in her life.

By the time the program was through, Jane had overcome her heroin addiction. Now in charge of her life, she was free of her addiction. She now had a fresh perspective on life and could anticipate a happy, healthy future.

Jane was appreciative of the Redemption program and pleased with herself for her successes. She had acquired the power to conquer her addiction and a fresh sense of independence. Her second opportunity had been granted to her through redemption, and she was determined to make the most of it.

Chapter 6

Recovery From Addiction

Jane has experienced a great deal in her life. She had experienced abuse, addiction, and sadness. But despite everything, she had discovered courage and optimism. She had put a lot of effort into improving her health and quality of life.

For Jane, it marked the beginning of a new adventure. She was prepared to restart her life at last. She had chosen to leave the metropolis and establish herself in a new location. She felt both excitement and apprehension.

She came to find quiet and tranquility as well as a warm welcome from her new neighbors. She moved into her new house right away and started getting acquainted with her surroundings. She was in awe of the area's beauty and the locals' friendliness.

Jane was committed to maximizing her new life. She decided to prioritize her physical and emotional well-being as well as to live a balanced and meaningful life. She started engaging in pursuits that made her happy and at ease. She began learning how to cook, participated in yoga courses, and went on long treks.

As the weeks and months passed, Jane started to experience feelings of fulfillment and direction. She had discovered a position that she liked and that allowed her to make ends meet. Additionally, she was able to begin forming deep bonds with her new friends and neighbors.

Jane was prospering a year later. Her physical and emotional health had much improved. She had a strong, certain feeling. She had come a long way and could proudly reflect on her past after having achieved so much progress.

Jane was now leading a life that was joyful and meaningful. She had accomplished her objectives and was already living the life she had always wanted. She was appreciative of all the changes that had come her way and were excited and hopeful about the future.

Jane's future was suddenly looking promising, and she was eager to see what the future held for her. She was prepared to take on new challenges, further her education, and learn new things. She was now pleased, happy, and enjoying a life of freedom. Jane was finally prepared to accept her new existence since this was it.

Chapter 7

Conclusion

Jane had made significant progress in her fight against drug addiction. She was committed to doing whatever it would take to recover now that she had made the initial steps toward acknowledging she had a problem.

It was difficult at first to resist desires and cravings and maintain sobriety. Jane needed to be on guard and enlist the aid of her loved ones, friends, and professionals. She put a lot of effort into creating a new, healthier lifestyle and often attended group meetings and therapy sessions.

With time, Jane's attitude and quality of life started to change. She delighted in simple pleasures like spending time with her grandchildren and taking walks in the countryside. She met new people and joined support groups, which gave her the willpower and inspiration to carry on.

After some time, Jane was allowed to leave her treatment center and go back to her house. She could now maintain employment and live a more independent life.

Even though she still had times of uncertainty and dread, she was committed to persevering and developing. She was content with her development and appreciative of all the help she had had along the road.

Jane had reached a state of tranquility and satisfaction. She had made significant progress in her fight against heroin addiction, and for the first time in a very long time, she felt hopeful about the future. After finding her way back, Jane was certain that she would continue living a better, happier life.